MANIPULATION

31 Powerful Techniques to Secretly Manipulate, Persuade and Influence People

LEONARD MOORE

MANIPULATION

TABLE OF CONTENTS

Free Bonus

3 Insanely Effective Words
To Hypnotize Anyone In A Conversation

If you're trying to persuade and convince other people then words are the most important tool you absolutely have to master.

As humans we interact with words, we shape the way we think through words, we express ourselves through words. Words evoke feelings and have the ability to talk to the listener's subconscious.

In this free guide you'll discover 3 insanely effective words that you can easily use to start hypnotizing anyone in a conversation.

Go to **www.eepurl.com/cRTY5X** to download the free guide

Introduction

Think of all the instances when you've been told "you'll do this if you really care about me" or "you'll lose me if you don't do this."

During the mid 20th century, a famous and powerful leader discovered the psychological impact of playing on people's emotions. He dedicated years to the art of mastering body language, theatrics, public speaking and using emotionally evocative words/phrases. His hand gestures, expressions and voice were near perfect for stirring the emotions he intended among the audience. His followers adored him, and were hooked to every word he uttered. In short, the leader had completely conquered the art of hypnotizing people through verbal and non-verbal skills during his public addresses.

Wondering who I am referring to? Yes, Adolf Hitler!

We manipulate and are manipulated on a daily basis. From small requests by co-workers to emotional blackmail by our partner, only the degree of manipulation differs. People knowingly or unknowingly are almost always trying to get others to do what they want them to do through a series of techniques. At times, on an extreme level, there is no regard for ethics or the other person's emotions. All that the manipulator intends to do is serve his purpose.

Manipulation is nothing but getting others to do exactly what you desire them to do without necessarily focusing on their good or desires. It has a negative undertone primarily because manipulation generally doesn't take the other person's well-being or interests into consideration. However there are exceptions to this.

It can be used positively to get someone who is otherwise non-receptive or stubborn to listen to you for their own good. It can be used for as a back hand technique for persuading and influencing people through charisma, misinformation, wordplay or even hypnotism.

The primary objective of manipulators is to lead people to do what you desire them to without them knowing that they are being manipulated to serve your purpose. You can also use it as a powerful tool for turning the tables and accomplishing a positive outcome when nothing else seems to be working.

For instance, let us say you've been working diligently and loyally in your organization for several years, and are due for a well-deserved promotion or salary hike. You've tried everything in the book to convince the top bosses that you indeed deserve more than you are getting currently. The employers are being stingy and not making an effort to recognize your efforts.

In such a scenario, you may have to resort to manipulation by creating an imaginary job offer that you're considering from a competitor, who is willing to pay you more and offering you a better position. This may or may not be true. You may be employing deception simply to get the miserly and unworthy employers to give you your due. Is manipulation so bad in this situation? Not really because you're using it to achieve a positive end result that isn't trampling on other people's rights or emotions. You are using it to stand up for your rights when nothing else seems to be working.

Manipulation can be used constructively and positively in a scenario where it is near impossible to break through a person's stubbornness and unreasonableness.

We've actually been practicing manipulation even before we began speaking. Notice how babies cry and throw a huge fit when they want to be fed, comforted, kept clean and be put to sleep. Toddlers will throw tantrums at public places if they can't have their favorite toy. At times, they will stop eating food until their demands are met. As teenagers, we manipulate the most attractive people to go out on a date with us. It's a never ending process.

Manipulation basically originates from a place where an individual believes that their needs and wants should be placed before everyone else's needs and wants. They are the epicenter of the universe, and everything and everyone revolves around what they desire. Manipulation can be given a more positive twist when it is used for aligning your needs as well as those of others.

Another difference between influence/persuasion and manipulation is that while the former happens at a more conscious level or within our realm of awareness, the latter occurs at a more subconscious level, which is what makes it so dangerous and insidious. It attempts to restructure your entire thought process, reality, ideas and feelings to accomplish the other person's objectives.

Manipulation can comprise everything from smooth seduction skills to body language to hypnotism mainly for distorting or challenging another person's sense of reality. The aim is to get people to think and act in a manner you want them to think and act.

Have you watched any of Shakespeare's popular ballads, Macbeth and Othello? Manipulation plays a huge role in the narrative of these stories. The master playwright has used trickery and manipulation as an element of demonstrating human weaknesses and ambition. The central plot or theme of these ballads is deception and manipulation. For instance, In Macbeth Lady Macbeth is shown to employ manipulative techniques to convince her husband into killing King Duncan and conquering the Scottish empire.

Finally, Macbeth launches into a maniacal murdering spree to protect himself, which leads to a bloodbath and eventually the death of both him and Lady Macbeth. The witch siblings and Lady Macbeth manipulate their way through the plot. They use underhand and sneaky methods to influence Lord Macbeth into doing horrific things that ultimately spell doom for everyone. They insidiously sow a tiny seed of ambition in Lord Macbeth that no one but he deserves to be on the throne. This leads to hostility between Duncan and Macbeth, and destruction of the empire.

Othello is another Shakespearean tragedy that uses the theme of manipulation. Lago, the wicked and sinister villain uses trickery and manipulation to dangerous seeds of suspicious in the mind of his master Othello against Othello's love Desdemona and Cassio, Othello's most loyal and trusted aide. Since Lago harbors the ambition of being the chief lieutenant, he devices an evil ploy to eliminate Cassio from the scene by leading Othello to suspect that Cassio is romantically involved with Desdemona and that both his trusted lieutenant and ladylove are betraying him. This is accomplished through a series of crafty tricks and especially created manipulative situations.

By creating a chain of events and circumstances, Lago injects suspicion, hatred and a feeling of revenge in Othello's mind. This leads to Othello killing his love Desdemona. Thus, through carefully orchestrated situations, words, non-verbal signals and actions, Lago successfully removes Cassio from the picture to take over his much-coveted position. Think about this – manipulation has been a part of our history and literature even before there was a term coined for it.

Yes, it has a low-brow and negative feel to it. However, it can also be used constructively to convince people about a good cause or get someone to do something for their own good, which they otherwise wouldn't do. When regular influence and persuasion techniques fail to work, manipulation may be the last resort.

Let us consider another example to understand how manipulation can be used to achieve positive means.

Imagine you have a childhood buddy Steve whose wife of several years just left him for another much younger man. Obviously, he is devastated. His teen children are left on their own, and Steve's entire life has come crashing down like a pack of cards. It is come as jolt of shock and unhappiness out of nowhere, sending him into deep depression.

You've learned through other common friends that Steve's entire life has come to a halt. He's not regular at work, and his productivity has taken a massive hit. Once a top worker within his organization, his performance has gone drastically down of late! According to friends and co-workers, he could be sacked soon.

As a friend, you are highly concerned about Steve. You are worried about the effects of his depression on Steve's personal and professional life. You gently urge him to seek professional help. In your opinion, therapy and counseling could bring his life back on the track. Since you know him since childhood, you know that Steve is a highly sensitive and emotional person who wouldn't take a betrayal like this very well.

However, Steve is not open to the idea of visiting a counselor or therapist because he doesn't believe it will solve his problem by getting back his wife. This is his opinion or perception. For him, the problem will only end once he gets his wife back. No other solution makes sense to him. You want him to get his life back and move on into a brighter future. But he refuses to give in, and is obstinate about his stand of not seeing a therapist. You employ every trick to convince, influence and persuade him. No result!

How do you then overcome this level of unreasonableness and stubbornness?

You are desperate now, and decide to use some below the table techniques to go past his obstinacy. So you fabricate this tale about a co-worker whose wife ditched him for another man, post which his life came tumbling down too. You launch into a cleverly crafted narrative about how it affected his personal life, and work performance. As someone who is using manipulation to accomplish a desired result, you attempt to use the right words, voice, expressions and gestures to communicate that your co-workers was a victim of depression.

You slowly inform Steve about how your co-worker decided enough is enough and sought the help of a therapist/counselor to grab the reins of his life once again. The co-worker started seeing a counselor recommended by you, and soon enough, there were positive changes in his life. With tactfulness, you inform Steve about how the co-worker gradually and successfully took control of his life. How he acquired the courage, positivity and hope to bounce back from a seemingly devastating situation!

You are simply attempting to stir the intended emotions in the person to get him to do something that is good for him or in his interest to move beyond his unreasonableness. After listening to the story, Steve decides to give counseling a chance. He is slightly moved by your narration of a person's triumph over his circumstances. Steve starts attending counseling and therapy sessions regularly. Gradually, his life begins to get normal. Steve appears to have gained greater control of his feelings and actions, which leads to increased productivity at work and a happier personal life.

None of what you told Steve is the truth. It is a spun story about an imaginary person. There was plenty of lies, deception, misinformation and trickery. However, was it bad? You manipulated your way into getting Steve to take action that is beneficial for me. You manipulated so that Steve would agree to see a therapist, when no other trick in the book worked. Sometimes, manipulation or trickery is the only opening you have to move past a person's unreasonableness to get them to take action in the intended direction.

Have you ever trained a pet? How do you get them to follow instructions such as "sit" "fetch" etc.? Yes, you'll most likely put their favorite treat before them and manipulate them into doing what you want if they wish to get the treat. It's called positive reinforcement. However, calling it training or positive reinforcement is clever wordplay. In its essence, it is similar to manipulation, albeit used to accomplish a positive outcome.

As parents, we manipulate our children into believing in Santa Claus, monsters and tooth fairies to get them to behave themselves or do things that are good for them. We all know eating spinach does not bestow them with any superpowers but that doesn't stop us from spinning tales to get an obstinate toddler to eat vegetables he or she dislikes. At times, deception and manipulation is the only way. You can use manipulation for helping people overcome bad habits, self-image issues, addiction and other issues. It can be used to change someone's life!

Manipulation is similar to a matchstick. In darkness, it can be used to light a candle. However, it can also be used to cause a devastating fire. We all have this tool of manipulation, which much like a hammer can be used to fix a nail in the wall or breakdown the entire wall. How you use this tool of manipulation is up to you – it can be both positive and negative.

Chapter One:
Foot in the Door Technique

Wondering about the rather amusing name this manipulation technique has acquired? It dates back to the era of door to door salespersons, where the sales people were believed to keep their foot in the door in a bid to avoid people from slamming their doors. Keeping their foot in the door apparently gave the opportunity to have more conversation with their prospective customers, and eventually clock a few sales.

How is 'foot in the door' used as a modern day manipulation technique?

You begin by establishing a rapport or breaking the ice with a person by requesting for something small. In effect, you are getting your foot in the door just to build a rapport with them so as to get them to do something bigger for you later. The initial request should be easy to meet. Don't ask for something big at the onset. Slowly and steadily, you can move in with a bigger or actually intended request very subtly.

You are attempting to launch into a series of favorable replies which has higher chances of ending with a "yes." This is exactly why psychologists and consumer behavior experts suggest that salespeople also ask questions to their prospective customers, where the customer replies only in the positive. According to a psychological research, if you can get potential customers to answer "yes" to six questions in a row, they are more likely to say "yes" to your product or service. This works on a highly subconscious and psychological level. Try it!

You launch into a series of positive responses, which makes it subconsciously near impossible for the other person to refuse the final or actually intended request. Once people starting responding to your request in the affirmative, it is challenging to break that pattern and reply in the negative.

This is what salespeople in olden times did. They put their foot in door and gave themselves those additional 2-3 minutes with their potential customers to build upon their sales pitch, and attempt to sell their products. Think of it in today's social, public or even personal setting. You are being offered a small opening, which you can use to get people to do what you want them to.

Let us consider an example to see how this persuasion tactic works. Judy is completing her science project, which needs her to create a solar system model. She requests her mom to help her make a rough design for the project. Her mom does the sketch and collects all the material required for Judy to make the model. Judy then requests her mother to glue the different pieces together, which she willingly does.

Eventually, Judy's mother ends up completing the entire project with very little input form Judy. She used the foot in the door technique rather than directly asking her mom to complete her project at the onset, which she knew would be refused.

This technique was first analyzed by Jonathan Freedman and Scott Fraser in in the mid-20th century. The objective is to get a person to agree to a small and simple request before asking a larger "yes."

The duo behind the technique discovered that once an individual agrees to a small request, their chances of replying in the affirmative are much higher than if you directly present the larger request. In the above example, Judy got her mother to complete the entire project by putting together various pieces by getting her to agree to a smaller request of helping her create a rough design. Eventually, Judy fulfilled her larger request. This may not have been possible had she asked her mother to do the project for her straight off the bat in the beginning.

When using the foot in the door technique, ensure that the request is tiny small enough so it is becomes tough for people to refuse it. All the same, it should be important enough to make the other person feel like they've been kind in responding to you. The request should be for a positive reason so that the other person feels it is worth their while. Also, it should be something that a person will voluntarily do with any external influences such as pressure, rewards or money.

Chapter Two:
Social Proof

There's no doubt man is a social animal, and is likelier to follow suit when they realize that others are doing it too. It's the bandwagon or trend effect, which works wonderfully well as a manipulation technique.

Since primitive times, man is wired to believe what everyone else is doing must be the best and right way to do things. The herd mentality seldom fails to work since it's so deeply embedded in our psyche. When you are invited to a social gathering, the first question you are likely to ask is who all are coming? You want to know whether the gathering is important enough for others to attend.

You will be likelier to attend once you realize that your friends or competitors are going to be there too. We fear being left out. There is this deep seated need to do things everyone else is doing.

Why do you think review sites such as Yelp are so popular? Why do companies request you to leave a review where everyone else can read them? It is all about social validation. You can get people to do what you want by offering them proof of how people similar to them are doing the same thing.

I once had a salesperson come to me for selling personalized children's storybooks. I refused to buy into that sort of a thing because I thought they were simply hyped and overpriced. I mean I am not going to shell out big bucks just for my child to see his or her name in print in the storybook. However, the salesperson was no rookie, and refused to take no for answer. He kept telling me I was free to make up my mind without any pressure, and yet telling me about Mr. so and so neighbor and Mr. so and so co-worker who had all purchased the books from him as special gifts for their children.

Really? Ah now let me think about this. Their kid loved it? Wow. They gifted their kid something that expensive? Why can't I? Why should my child be deprived from enjoying such a wonderful surprise when everyone else is enjoying it? Works like a charm!

Be honest, aren't you influenced to buy a product when it bags more positive reviews or buyers have rated it highly? You are likelier to buy something when other people similar to you validate it. If a friend recommends a movie, restaurant and book, you are likelier to pick it up. That is the power of social proof.

People are constantly living under the fear and insecurity of being left out, which can be utilized cleverly to get them to make immediate decisions. Social proof is one of the smartest and most effective manipulation and persuasion strategy.

Positive or negative, people are prone to listen to other people. This how fads and trends begin! Create or present social proof demonstrating that others are doing it too if you want to get a person to do something. They are insecure about being left out, don't forget that.

Chapter Three:
Establishing Similarity

This is probably one of the most powerful manipulation techniques because it works on a subconscious level. People almost always take to or believe people who they perceive to be similar to them. It goes back to the primordial hunter gatherer times, when human beings established their similarity or affiliation to each other through non-verbal signals.

Establishing similarly is effective and relevant in modern psychological persuasion and influence studies. Focus on creating similarity and familiarity if you want to get people to do what you say. This can be done carefully through your words, voice and body language.

Mirroring is a powerful tool when it comes to establishing similarity if you've only just met someone. This improves your chances of getting a person to trust you and do what you say. For example, if someone is leaning against the bar, slowly and subtly mirror their actions and lean against the bar. If the person raises his/her glass to sip on their drink, follow suit by taking a sip from your glass. Observe a person's words, mannerism and body language. What are the typical words they use? How is the tone, pitch and volume of their speech?

Employ the same verbal and non verbal communication patterns to demonstrate you are one among them at a subconscious level.

However, ensure that you are doing it very subtly and tactfully. If it's blatant, they'll think you are mocking or imitating them, which will harm your cause. This can work on everyone from a potential client to a hot new date you're trying to woo. Attempt to mirror everything from their words to their posture to their expressions and intonation.

This works on a very deep psychological level. When you mirror someone's verbal and non-verbal patterns, you reinforce the idea that you are one of them. This is especially helpful during business negotiations or if you are trying to persuade someone to go out on a date with you. They will subconsciously form a powerful sense of affiliation with you, and are likelier to do what you want them to.

Chapter Four:
Creating Scarcity

This is another general human tendency. We tend to perceive something that is scarce as more valuable. There is a higher value attached to things that aren't easily available or present in abundance. This is how price of goods and services is impacted by demand and supply. Something that is short in supply tends to be more expensive than something that is easily or abundantly available. This manipulation technique is used brilliantly by brand managers, marketers, promoters and advertisers to peddle their products.

Haven't we all heart "limited edition" "exclusive pieces" and "last few left" and more? It is nothing but a manipulation strategy to create a sense of scarcity for leading potential customers to take quick action in their insecurity and fear. When you pitch something as rare, unique or scarce, people are prone to act with a sense of urgency. They operate from the point that there isn't enough for everyone, and they'll be left out if they don't grab the offer/product/service soon.

When you wish to get people to take immediate action, simply create a feeling of scarcity. Focus on how something is available in very few numbers, and the customer stands to lose it to someone else if they don't act fast because there isn't enough for everyone. Play on this inherent feeling of insecurity that people possess, of not wanting to be left behind or lose something to someone else. Plus, scarcity makes the product or service more coveted. You reinforce that only a select few will be fortunate enough to enjoy the product or service.

If you want to get someone to take action in a specific direction, project the thing, service or anything else related to the intended action as scarce or available in short supply or for a limited period of time. It will immediately change a person's mindset related to that thing, and everyone will be clamoring to buy it.

Chapter Five:
Playing the Blame Game or Inducing Guilt

Emotional manipulators often play the victim's role to manipulate their victims into thinking that it is always their (the victim's) fault. Irrespective of who is responsible, they will always assign blame on the other person. This is done to shift responsibility from their shortcomings to make the other person feel guilty. When the victim feels guilty or blames himself/herself for the unfortunate situation, it is easier to get them to do what you want.

As a manipulator, you focus on how someone made you do something or how it was someone else's fault for which you are suffering. It is always other people who are angering or upsetting you. You don't accept any accountability for your actions.

For instance, let us say you forget your best friend's birthday. Predictably, your best friend is upset with you for forgetting her birthday. The logical thing to do is apologize and make up for it later. However, if you are a manipulative person, you resort to blame games and in turn blame your friend for making you feel so bad about forgetting their birthday. You'll induce a sense of guilt within the person to get them to do the intended thing.

You will most likely talk about how you've been stressed, busy and anxious of late, which has made it almost important to remember anything. To top it all, instead of supporting you, your friend is upset with you for something as trivial as forgetting his/her birthday. See what you are doing there? You are making the person feel guilty for a perfectly reasonable expectation. You are turning the tables on him or her to avoid the blame, and to get them to do what you want them to.

Manipulators don't just stop there. If you want to take it a step ahead, you will recount all the instances where your friend has forgotten important occasions. You are doing nothing but justifying that it is indeed their fault that they expected you to wish them a happy birthday on their birthday.

Master manipulators know how to invoke a sense of guilt within their victims to stirring these people into taking the desired action. They will use guilt and blame game masterfully to meet their own agenda.

For example, let us say that a person brings up an issue that is playing on their mind for a while. As a manipulator or persuader, you make them experience a sense of guilt for making such an issue out of what is in effect an absolute non-issue.

Thus instead of accepting the grievance and promising to work on it, you turn the tables on the other person and make them the guilty party for even bringing up the issue. People use this emotional manipulation tactic in personal relationships all the time.

So, as an emotional manipulator or persuader, you get a person to feel guilty about anything he or she does. If they don't talk, emotional manipulators blame them for not sharing their feelings. If they share their feelings too much, they will be blamed for creating issues where none exist. You keep stirring guilt in the other person regardless of their thoughts and actions to serve your purpose.

Whatever the other person does is attributed to them or seen as their fault, until they comply with your demands. All the same, you play the wronged victim. Creating a feeling of guilt is one of the strongest techniques for getting a person to obey your demands. This is even more effective on people who possess a low self esteem or low level of self confidence.

For instance, if you want to someone to do something for you, mention a list of all the things you've done for them or to help them. Then, follow this up with how they've let you down each time. So here, you become the projected victim who kept doing things for them in a bid to help them, and they become the ungrateful creatures who never stand up to the occasion when you need them.

Manipulators often get their partner to do what they desire by saying things such as, "it's absolutely alright Rachael, I can't really expect more from you. It's all my fault that I expected a lot from you and this relationship." This makes the other person feel like he or she is letting your down, and that you can never expect better from them, which in turn can induce a strong sense of guilt within them.

Ever notice how in our personal relationships we are playing manipulators and inducing guilt in our loved ones all the time? Notice how seniors make their children feel guilty about never having enough time for them. They seldom fail to remind their children that they won't be around for too long and it's unfortunate that their offspring can't spend enough time with them.

Also, when teenagers seek their parents' permission for overnight trips and slumber parties, and the parents refuse, notice how the teen will go on and on about how overprotective and suffocating the parents are to not allow him/her to explore the world on his/her own.

I am sure by now you have identified at least one person you know who blames victim all the time and unfailingly assigns blame on others. They will use their perceived helplessness as a tool for making others do what they want them to. As manipulator, you are giving other people the impression that they are determining your fate, and through their actions they've impacted your fate negatively. Now, it is up to them to make up for the damage they've done.

The victims will often start believing that they are responsible for the situation you are in, and are likelier to respond positively to your request. They will feel guilty about saying no to you. You project yourself as someone who needs help, and who is doomed if not helped. People feel bad, and do what you intend them to because they invariably end up feeling responsible for your situation and helplessness.

Chapter Six:
Using the Fear-Relief Cycle

This is another popular manipulation and persuasion technique that can be used in almost any scenario or setting, and is especially exploited by advertisers and marketers for convincing their target audience to buy their products or services. Again, it works on a deeply psychological level, which makes it highly effective.

This manipulation technique involves preying on the fears of consumers to get them to do what you want them to. Induce a sense of fear in the person, and once they imagine the worst, follow it up with relief. They'll experience a huge surge of positive emotions that will help them make a decision in your favor.

Let us consider an example. You can say something such as, "When I put on your sandals for the prom night, I heard a terrible sound of the footwear giving away. I was dead sure it snapped. Then, I realized someone was watching a video on their phone. Isn't that amusing? Oh and this reminds me, may I please borrow the pair of sandals again for an upcoming weekend party?"

You did nothing but took the person through a cycle of fear and relief to end on a positive note. In the above example, there is immediate relief that the sandals are in great condition. The other person gets into a more positive and receptive mental frame, which makes it easier to get them to do what you want.

You begin by sowing the seeds of fear about the worst that can happen in a situation. This is then followed up by offering a solution or launching into a narrative about how things were far less worse than the other person imagined (as in example of the sandal).

On a psychological level, the victim experiences a cycle of strong emotions. The fear gets them uncomfortable, anxious and nervous. This is followed by immediate hope, positivity and relief.

Let us consider another example of how this manipulation strategy works. Almost all life insurance salespersons play on this fear-relief cycle to make sales. They induce fear, anxiety and panic related to the well-being of your loved ones after you pass away. Then introduce a 'simple' solution – purchasing a policy that ensures your loved ones are financially secure enough to look after themselves when you aren't around to provide for them. This little trick instills a sense of hope, security and relief in the person, and leads them to make a purchasing decision.

Children use this trick several times when they want to communicate something seemingly not so good to their parents. For instance, they may say something such as, "I flunked the Math test mom." When they notice the parent is visibly upset or angry, they'll quickly add, "Hey it's not so bad, I got a B." The parent who was expecting an A won't feel so bad after all because it is still better in comparison to the information shared by the child earlier (flunking). Thus, the parent doesn't feel too terrible about the "B" even though she may have otherwise rebuked the child if he had straight off mentioned that he'd got a "B" instead of a better grade.

There are experiments mentioned in *The Science of Social Influence*, which will establish the fear-relief technique. In one such experiment, mall visitors were alarmed at being tapped on the shoulder from behind by strangers. When people turned, they discovered a blind man who requested to know the time.

After the fear, the blind person's associates would go ahead and ask people to buy postcards and sign them for a charitable cause. This rollercoaster or whirlwind of emotions got people to buy the postcards, which they may have otherwise not done. The feeling of relief right after an increased sense of fear ended up making them feel positive, and in turn help them take the intended action.

This is also a technique used by investigators popularly known as the bad cop, good cop technique. A law enforcement authority will induce fear in a suspect, while another one will come over and pretend to rescue him or her or be a good cop. This way the suspect is more receptive to sharing information with the good cop.

Notice how your manager plays on the fear relief technique by telling you that the company is downsizing and laying off people. Then, they'll add that you can keep your job if you put in additional hours at work for a few weeks or the only thing that can save your job is doing overtime.

Chapter Seven:
Use the Home Ground Advantage

If you want to get someone to do what you want or convince/persuade/influence them into doing something, always insist that they come to your home, office or any other space. This is again a psychological and subconscious advantage you are giving yourself when it comes to influencing people. The theory behind this is simple. When you negotiate in a physical space that you own, you are in your territory, which gives you a subconscious advantage. It can be any place you are familiar with – from your office to garage to home to car. Network and chain marketers almost always attempt to gain the home court advantage. They will invite their prospects to come over to their place for a meeting or presentation. You'll seldom find them accepting a request to come over to your place to give you a presentation.

You have an upper hand over the other person or are in an authoritative position to call the shots and get them to comply with your request. This is a little known social manipulation secret that people aren't aware of. When you are in your physical space or territory, you are able to wield greater control, dominance and influence compared to the other person. Subconsciously, you both realize that you exercise greater power here. This in turn reflects not just on your attitude but also words, body language and actions.

If you are negotiating an important deal or finalizing the terms for an important association, insist that the other person come over into your home or office for a chat. Somehow, make them come into your territory to gain a psychological edge over them. This will increase your chances of getting them to do what you want them to. The comfort, ease and familiarity of your space will put you in a better position and give you more confidence, thus boosting your chances of sealing the deal to your advantage.

Explain to a person that they need to understand everything clearly, which is why they should come over to your place to know all details. This is your reasoning for them. Actually, you are only giving yourself a more authoritative edge by holding negotiations in your physical space.

Chapter Eight:
Creating A False Sense of Intimacy

This is another powerful manipulation technique that aims to gain a subject's trust by creating a false sense of intimacy. This is done by sharing something personal that makes the other person be misled into believing that they can trust you. They drop down their guard, and are more receptive to what you are saying once they trust you. This is especially true with people who are more suspicious of others. It lowers a person's defenses and helps to get them to open up a little. Creating a false sense of intimacy works wonders.

How does one move past this trust barrier? Ensure the information you share is slightly personal and confidential that you wouldn't just share with anyone. Of course, it shouldn't be something very personal or secretive. Just something that is personal enough for the subject to feel valued about you sharing this piece of information with them. This makes the person lower their guard and trust you.

Share something that they can connect with or relate to. It can also be something that is important to know. The information may be real or made up. The point is to make it come across as genuine to win the person's trust.

If a person has been manipulated a few earlier, he/she will be unlikely to trust people. If trust is the biggest barrier when it comes to getting the person to do what you want, kill it by sharing private with the subject. Your focus is on winning the subject's trust so they demonstrate faith in you. Again, make your act look genuine to gain credibility and the subject's trust.

Chapter Nine:
Master Debating and Public Speaking Skills

Manipulation is all about being charming and building lots of charisma to sweep the other person off their feet into doing what you want them to. It is almost similar to hypnotizing the person through your aura, persona and charm. When you speak charmingly and articulately, it is easier to get people to perform the desired action. Yes, having a glib tongue and being a smooth talker helps when it comes to manipulating people. Sign up for a public speaking or theatre class if you really want to be a master influencer or persuader.

You will not just learn to put across your point in a more impactful and persuasive manner but also come across as more confident, which will help the subject trust your words even more. Assertiveness and not aggression is the key to being a good influencer. You'll learn to out across your point more assertively and confidently. Some of the best manipulators know how to use verbal and non verbal communication patterns to their advantage. They can mold everything from their words to voice to expressions to assume a more persuasive, powerful and confident persona.

Just imagine you are in a room full of people. Suddenly two people enter. One has an awkward, inhibited and meek body language, while the other looks confident, self-assured and powerful. Who do you think will be noticed? Of course, the one with an imposing persona! People invariably sit up and notice those with a strong persona. You'll be a people magnet if you learn to present your ideas more compellingly and convincingly.

To enhance your theatrics, speech and drama skills (you'll need plenty of those if you want to be a master manipulator), sign up for a drama workshop. The greatest challenge when it comes to manipulating or influencing people is to have control over your emotions! At times, you'll even have to fake emotions (remember the example about Steve in the introduction?). You also need to manage your body language, speech and voice to invoke the desired reaction in your subjects.

If you want to generate specific feelings and emotions in people, you've got to gain control of your body language, expressions, posture, gestures and more. Observe the way professional actors emote. Study their mannerisms, expressions and dialogue delivery. Notice the way they use their voice tone to create the required impact on the audience.

At times, they'll say something very critical and pause for a while to allow what they've just said to have the desired impact. This gives you a brief idea of how you should prepare yourself for being the ultimate manipulator and influencer.

At times, you may be really glad or elated that the person has agreed to do what you desire them to. However, you may have to restrain your emotions or not make it too conspicuous. Manipulating or controlling speech, gesture, posture, expressions and voice requires skill and practice. You may have to create certain emotions and expressions to get what you want. How about manipulating or faking certain emotions even when you don't feel it. Say for instance acting dejected when you don't get something or cry at the drop of a hat.

Observe the histrionics of a salesperson. Their body language, speech and expressions are exaggerated to produce the desired result.

Chapter Ten:
Mastering Body Language for Influencing People

Body language is an important aspect of non verbal communication, which is exactly the reason why people generally insist on in person meetings when they have to discuss something important. There is a need to note a person's expressions, gestures, posture, voice tone and more to know more about how they feel from within.

Here are some power-packed tips for influencing and manipulating people with the help of body language.

Keep your body language confident, self-assured and assertive. If your body language appears hesitant, inhibited, full of self-doubt and sloppy, there's little chance people are going to take you seriously. Always keep an upright posture. Keep your arms and legs uncrossed while talking to people. Your palms should stay open most of the time. Maintain a relaxed yet confident posture if you want people to trust you.

Always lean towards the other person while talking to show your interest in them. Tilt your head in their direction. Maintain a distance though, and don't thrust your face on theirs! Point your feet towards the subject's direction since it reveals interest and attention. Avoid invading a person's private space by getting too physically close to them too soon or they are less likely to trust you. Tilt your body slightly towards their direction or lean over a table to demonstrate your interest.

To create an instant rapport with a person, always align your body language with theirs. Face the person directly while speaking to reveal your interest and attention. This makes you come across as more affable, likeable and attentive, which in turn helps build a favorable rapport with the other person. This is even truer when you are communicating with a single person within a group setting. If you want to demonstrate interest in a person, face the person directly and align your body language with his or her body language. This will make them more receptive to what you say.

Always look a person right in the eye while speaking. Maintain eye contact throughout your communication with them. Shifting your gaze away from them frequently will make you come across as deceitful and dishonest. Similarly, from the person occasionally, but in general keep your gaze fixated on them while talking.

Stay attentive, interested and relaxed. Don't fidget with your fingers, tap your feet or play with objects. It gives the message that you are disconnected or disinterested in what the person is saying. These are also signs of nervousness. Let your hands and legs stay in a relaxed position.

When it comes to winning people, nothing works its charm as effectively as a smile. It is a wonderful ice-breaker and allows you to build a rapport with the other person on a subconscious level. Have a smile permanently fixed on your face while talking to people. It boosts your likeability factor.

A great tip for enhancing your body language when it comes to influencing, persuading and manipulating people is practice before a mirror. It lets you determine how you look while speaking to and interacting with other people. You can make the required changes to appear more influential and persuasive.

Observe closely your expressions, postures, tone, gestures, words and voice while speaking. Does it have the intended effect on a person? Does your confidence and conviction come across while talking to a person? Does your speech influence others into taking immediate action? Are people inspired by what you say?

Another powerful technique for observing your body language, expressions, gestures and voice is to record important presentations, negotiations and meetings. Closely examine your body language at these meetings. Do you come across as persuasive, convincing and forceful in your communication? Do you inspire other people's trust and conviction through your body language? This way you can make the necessary changes for altering your communication pattern to make it even more impactful.

Each time you are introduced to someone, demonstrate confidence and authority subconsciously through a firm handshake. Don't crush the person's hand or you'll come across as aggressive, and don't offer a limp handshake, which makes you appear unsure, low on confidence and inhibited. Stick to a handshake that is establishes your confidence and assertiveness.

Use power poses to your advantage. Social psychologist Amy Cuddy has spoken at length about how specific power poses help elevate our body's testosterone levels, and lower the stress inducing cortisol levels in as little as two minutes. These poses have a direct bearing on how we think and feel. Generally, these poses comprise forming broader body postures or occupying greater space or making your frame appear huge. By occupying greater physical space, you firmly establish yourself as a more authoritative and powerful person subconsciously.

Widen your stance slightly while standing so that your feet are apart. This makes you come across as a more powerful and confident personality. If you keep your feet firmly closely held together, you come across as insecure, nervous and anxious, which isn't very effective when it comes to influencing people.

Use your hands to enhance your speech. Brain research has pointed to the fact that the brain's broca region, which is significant for speech generation is stimulated when we use our hands or wave in an animated manner. Therefore, speech production and gestures are inextricably connected. Thus, we facilitate our words, thoughts, ideas and expressions through the use of hand gestures, making us even more effective communicators. Try to use your hands in animated gestures throughout the speech to improve the quality of your content significantly. You speech will possess better clarity and more impactful words/expressions.

Chapter Eleven:
Present Information and Statistics

Emotional manipulation doesn't work very effectively with logical or rational people, especially in professional settings. Some people are more inclined to trust logical arguments and statistics more than a tug at their heart strings. Drown these people in information, facts, numbers and statistics.

If you are presenting a specific viewpoint or want people to think along the intended direction, have your facts ready. Fight objections with statistics. Present them cleverly to make your case stronger. It is termed as intellectual bullying. Be the expert source of knowledge in a specific domain. Smartly present research and ideas that support your view. If you have established expertise in a field, utilize it to the fullest.

Concentrate on areas where you think you possess good knowledge and question your subject about it. Make their weaknesses obvious so you can use these weaknesses to fulfill your purpose.

Manipulators work on people's fear by blowing facts out of proportion or context. They will sneakily highlight only certain aspects of a research to induce a sense of fear in people. For instance, let us say a man doesn't want his partner to pursue a career, and wants her instead to focus on the home and children. He may cleverly say something like, "research has found in 70 percent of all separations and divorces that happen, both partners are involved in full-time jobs."

Reasons other than the woman's full time job are smartly hidden to present that as the only cause of destruction of the institution of marriage. This is done with the intention of preying on the woman's insecurity of losing the man or relationship at the cost of her ambitions. It can be made to work on an emotional level albeit with the use of facts to back up your stand. When you convince a person with information and statistics that support your stand, your chances of getting a person to do what you want them to increase!

This method works well in all scenarios from debates to sales to business negotiations and personal relationships. By drowning them in information, you give yourself a subconscious edge. The other person becomes defenseless and more receptive to listening. You become intellectually superior, while they feel inadequate and unarmed, which makes them more open to listening to you! Notice how salespeople and network marketers use statistics to their advantage all the time.

They tell you how, "80 percent of the people are dissatisfied with their job and seek more time and money freedom" or "60 percent men in the age group of 30-60 die due to a sudden heart attack, which leaves their family stranded, which is why you must have life insurance."

Chapter Twelve:
Rationalization or Making Excuses

Rationalization is a manipulation technique where a manipulator or persuader offers some kind of rationale or justification for his offensive and inappropriate behavior. This one is the toughest to spot because the reasons given seem so plausible that the subject buys it almost immediately. It makes sense to the other person, which makes it so effective.

Rationalizing fulfills three main purposes including removing any resistance that the subject may have towards the manipulator, keeping other people from blaming the manipulator and justifying the manipulator's acts in the eyes of the subject.

It may be used for justifying ethically, morally, legally or socially incorrect behavior. For instance a person may have an affair outside their marriage and may justify their act by saying how they are caught in an unhappy marriage instead of working on the marriage. They may blame their spouse for "leading them to the affair" This is a typical rationalization manipulation behavior.

People who resort to the rationalization technique will typically act in an erratic manner. They tend to be affectionate suddenly, while at other times they are cold. When the subject airs their grievances, the manipulator will justify their acts by stating how they've been depressed and stressed lately. How their work is taking a toll on their health and well-being. They will behavior insensitively yet they will create a strong justification for their unpredictable behavior. It works because its spun in way that it does seem logical.

At times, as a manipulator you will move people by stating how you're going through a tough situation in life or how stressful your life is currently. To be a manipulator, you've got to be a wonderful performer, and play the rationalization card with ease. Justify your acts using everything from circumstances to people to other things beyond your control.

Chapter Thirteen:
Gaslighting

Gaslighting has found its way in Hollywood movies and literature and as a well-known manipulation technique. It is a hidden manipulation strategy where the manipulator seeks to twist facts or reality to suit his or her agenda. It consists of misleading the subject to believe that their perception of reality isn't true, and this is purely their fault. The idea that they aren't able to view things as they are is so deeply ingrained in the person's psyche that he/she actually begins to doubt their thinking. Their notion of reality is challenged to serve the manipulator's purpose.

So as a manipulator, you use your verbal and non verbal manipulation skills to get the other person to accept your version of reality. This is one of the most insidious forms of manipulation and must be used with caution because it comprises making the subject feel mentally incompetent enough to think right. You get them to stop having faith in themselves so they can have faith in you and implicitly trust everything you say.

The technique is commonly used by dictators, cult leaders and abusers to prevent the victim from realizing that he/she has been completely brainwashed. The term is derived from the 1944 film *Gaslight* where a man manipulates his spouse to such an extent that she starts thinking she's losing her sanity.

Manipulators who use the gaslighting technique typically lie blatantly, and with a straight face. They'll tell one big lies and their subjects aren't sure if it is a lie or truth. This is done to keep their victims unsteady and unsettled. Gaslighting involves outright denial of having said something, even with the subject has sufficient proof. It makes the victim question his own sense of reality when manipulators lie blatantly. Maybe the person didn't say it after all. The manipulator keeps building on this so questioning your sense of reality becomes a pattern until you stop accepting your version of reality and begin accepting theirs!

Master manipulators who use manipulation for negative purposes will often identify things a person values the most. It can be everything from your kids to your identity. As a manipulator, you identify a person's weaknesses and attack them first. You tell the person he or she would be a worthy person if they didn't have an extended list of negative attributes. By saying all this, you directly hit the foundation of a person's existence. This is a complicated technique where you are constantly being unpredictable to throw the person off guard or challenge their notion of reality.

At times, you praise the subject for something they did. This creates a greater sense of uneasiness. The subject begins thinking that you aren't that bad. This is a carefully calculated strategy to keep the subject confused and mentally inadequate. It attempts to question their sense of reality. Praise them especially for something that serves their purpose.

Gaslighters are aware that their actions create a sense of instability. Their goal is to uproot subjects and make them perpetually question everything. And when you feel a strong sense of instability or lack of balance, you lean on another person. This is exactly what the gaslighter wants. They want their subjects to be unsure of themselves so they can then lean on the manipulator for stability, which will make them more receptive to doing what the manipulator wants them to.

Chapter Fourteen:
Following Up an Unreasonable Request with a Reasonable One

This is another brilliant psychological manipulation, persuasion strategy that works wonders. We use it in our everyday lives knowingly or unknowingly to get people to do what we want. It is complicated, and yet effective because it plays on a psychological level.

You start by making a highly unreasonable request that is tough for the other person to meet. This is followed by a more practical or reasonable request or what you actually want the other person to do. The way it works is — the subject will compare your initial unreasonable request against the more doable one and arrive at the conclusion that the second one is easy to tackle. It is tough to refuse a person more than once, especially if he/she has reduced his request the second time.

The subject will most likely be alright with the second request in comparison to the first. They'll feel like you've come halfway and be compelled to come halfway themselves. The first request will suddenly through them off gear. Later, they will feel much more psychologically comforted with the later request. This cycle of feelings and emotions can work well in your favor as an influencer and manipulator.

Lets us consider an example to better illustrate this point. Let us say you want leave for a couple of days in the middle of an important assignment because something urgent has come up. You know if you ask your boss straight to be away from work for two days in the middle of an insanely busy period, he'll refuse hands down. He will rebuke your professionalism and attitude towards work for even coming up with such a lousy suggestion.

However, if you ask him for 15 days leave, he will be raging. Your manager will think you are out of your mind to even come up with such as insane and unreasonable request. There's no chance he is going to grant you 15 days leave.

Pretend to be slightly disappointed and immediately follow it up with your actual request. The manager will weigh your initial request of 15 days against the 2 day leave, and find that you've really come down from your initial request, which makes you come across as someone who has compromised for the sake of the company. This makes your actual request hard to refuse. For added measure, you can also speak about making up for the lost hours by working extra for the next few days. Now, this is almost impossible to beat! Once someone says no to you for something, it becomes tough for them to say no to next request, especially if it happens to be smaller in comparison to the earlier request.

Chapter Fifteen:
Goal Post Moving and Nitpicking

There is a difference between positive or constructive criticism and negative criticism. From a negative manipulation point of view, manipulators come up with near impractical or impossible to meet standards, so they hold an upper hand on their subjects. Once you have an upper hand on the subject by pretending to help them, you can get them to do what you want. You have to act like you truly have their best intention in mind while constantly nitpicking. As a manipulator, you may have to pretend to have the person's best interests in mind while moving the goal post all the time.

Moving goal posts is nothing but never being short of reasons to be disillusioned or disappointed with the other person to get them to do what you want them to. Covert manipulation experts are adept in the technique of coming up with new goals and constantly making their disappointment with people obvious. Even when their request is fulfilled or the subject stands validated, the manipulator will come up with another unreasonable request just to create a constant sense of inadequacy in a person.

As a manipulator, you constantly ask the other person to prove something.

For instance, let us say you start by picking on a person for not being physically active. Once they are physically active, you question them for not being a successful professional. Once they accomplish reasonable success in their careers, you ask them why they aren't millionaires yet. Then, you focus on why they can't maintain a balance in their personal and professional life. You keep changing goals constantly so the person feels inadequate about himself or herself.

Again, this may be a negative manipulation technique and needs to be used with discretion because you are making the other person feel incompetent and playing on their sense of unworthiness to fulfill your agenda. Constructive or positive manipulation will comprise offering positive criticism to help the person overcome his or her shortcomings.

However, negative manipulation involves growing people's limitations to make them feel powerless. Genuine persuaders and influencers don't instill a feeling of unworthiness in their subjects. They will suggest multiple ways to overcome or resolve the issue. The constructive criticism is disguised simply as nitpicking without giving any tangible solutions.

If a person keeps demanding more proof for validating your argument or keeps raising their expectations, their aim is obviously not to understand you better. They are attempting to provoke you into experiencing a sense of inadequacy or that you have to keep proving yourself all the time.

Chapter Sixteen:
Use the Power of Stories

Stories work wonderfully well when it comes to putting across your point in a convincing and persuasive manner because they have a human element attached to them. Don't we all love teachers who tell stories to illustrate an idea or lesson? What about speakers who narrative comprises interesting anecdotes and stories? Gets us hooked right? People buy stories because there is something human about it that touches their heart or they can relate to over plain mechanical facts. Anyone can go on and on about facts.

However, narrating stories and anecdotes is an art that will help you build a rapport with your subjects when it comes to manipulating or influencing them to do what you want them to.

Stories set the tempo for a discussion or talk. Include lots of real life example that the subject can relate to. If you are talking to potential customers about purchasing a product or service, narrate a real life example about how the product or service made someone's life better or easier. Similarly, if you are trying to reiterate a principle or values, use fictional stories. They work well for self-help and motivational/ inspirational talks as well.

Keep it simple and relatable. The lesson should be easy to absorb. You should be able to generate the right feelings and emotions in people through the narration. It should appeal to both, the person's sense of logic and emotion. Sometimes, it isn't easy to evoke the right emotions in people simply by telling them about it. Stories and examples make it more compelling because they speak at level where the person can identify with the characters.

You can use it during business presentations, negotiations, sales or even to break the ice with someone you've just met. Imagining narrating a funny story about friend to establish rapport with someone you've just met. You come across as a friendly, funny and light-hearted person who is interesting and can make others laugh. This puts you in a better position when it comes to getting people to do what you want them to. I tell the most powerful stories while chatting informally with clients over a cup of coffee. In any situation, they seldom fail to weave their charm.

To make your stories more impactful, keep the relevant, simple, brief and meaningful. The lesson or gist of your narrative should be easy to absorb. Of course, it isn't just the story that will make an impact but also the way in which you narrate it. This is where your theatrics, body language, public speaking skills and speech will come into play. Try to connect with your listeners by developing your verbal and non-verbal communication skills.

Take your audience through a whirlwind of emotions by slowly and clearly narrating as story. Know when to pause for effect so the magnitude of what you are trying to say sinks in.

Ensure that you story strikes a chord with your target audience. It should resonate with their primary ideas, beliefs, values, lifestyle and other factors. Don't talk about narratives they can barely relate to. This will make your point across as something that is relevant to them or meant for them. Similarly, don't fill the story with too many characters or esoteric ideas that are difficult to gasp. People don't like to think too much about abstract concepts. Their attention span is limited, and they'll quickly switch off.

An effective persuasion story is one that uses uncomplicated symbolism which is easily understood by the audience. You want to get your point or message across in a compelling manner and not hide it in the veil of complex symbolism and abstract ideas.

Chapter Seventeen:
Know Your Subject's Interests

The main idea of this manipulation or persuasion technique is to know what exactly the other person wants and giving it to them. For instance, you identify the main interests of the person so you can use this knowledge for hooking them into a conversation for building rapport.

Did you know that high end car salespeople are actually trained to peep inside their prospect's car to make a note of their (the prospect's) interests so the salesperson can then build a conversation around it establish a rapport with the potential customers? For instance, if a salesperson spots a golf kit inside the car, he/she can launch into a conversation about how they love playing golf during weekends or they have to leave early today because they have a golf tournament lined up.

When the customer who is passionate about golf or plays golf notices someone talk about his/her interests or share his/her interests, he/she immediately feel a sense of affinity for the same. He/she is similar to me because he/she shares my interests. He/she is friendly, likeable and approachable because he/she likes the same things I do.

Initially, you will have to make an effort to know what the person likes or his/her interests. Look at his/her social media foot prints to know the type of pages they follow, the type of posts they react to or what they post. It will give you a good grip of the person's beliefs, values and interests. Similarly, converse with the person in an informal manner (even if is a business or professional associate) to understand his or her interests.

Try to understand what their likes and dislikes are, and keep building upon it to hook them to do what you want them to. The best way to find out people's interests is to ask them how they spend their free time. This will also give you a good idea about the individual's personality or values. If they say something about watching television or Netflix during their free time, you know you are dealing with a slightly lazy and physically inactive person who is passive consumer of entertainment or information.

Someone else may add they love working out or running in their free time. This is most likely a driven, goal-oriented and ambitious person who loves results and staying active. They are highly motivated. What a person does in his/her free time can give you several clues about not just their interests but the type of people they are. I once met a person for the first time at a party and posed this question to her.

She told me she loved volunteering for an NGO during her free time. This gave me a good glimpse of the altruistic style, and made it easier for me to appeal to her humanitarian side for the purpose of getting her to do what I wanted her to. When you know what people want and what drives them, it becomes easier to play on it.

People are interested in various things. If you can exchange ideas or talk to them about their pet interests, you develop an instant rapport with them or come across as more likeable.

Chapter Eighteen:
Listen, Listen and Listen

Contrary to what most people mistakenly perceive, communication and influencing people is not just about talking. A major chunk involves listening to people. When you listen to people, you come across as attentive and interested in them, which makes you instantly likeable in their eyes. Don't we all like people who give us their full attention and listen to us keenly over people who just talk nineteen to a dozen about irrelevant things? Communication is as much about listening to people as it is about putting your point across effectively.

When you listen, you establish a level of trust that is hard to beat. Plus, by listening you understand a person's innermost desires, triggers, values, interests, beliefs, personality and much more, which can be used in your favor to get them to do what you want. Hence listening serves a dual purpose. It gives the other person an impression that you are attentive towards and interested in what they saying. Plus, it gives you a good idea about the person to build on this knowledge.

When you listen to people keenly, you are also better armed to come up with effective responses. Say for instance, you are trying to sell something to someone. And the person objects to the price in comparison with another company's product. You don't catch the word price because you haven't been listening keenly to the person. You only hear the competitor's name and launch into a verbose narrative about how the company operates at an unethical level, and how their products are not up to the mark and more. This may or may not be relevant to the customer's concerns.

If you would've simply listened keenly to the customer, you would've noted that their real object is the high price of your product. Once you would've realized that price is the real concern, you would've explained how your product or service offers much better value than several competitors in the market. You would've focused on the customer's real concern rather than the bringing up the drivel about your competitor's reputation, which isn't the customer's real concern.

We hear things only half-heartedly and jump to respond without even attempting to understand what the other person is trying to say. Sometimes, we take it a step ahead by preparing our responses while the person is speaking without understanding where he or she is coming from. When you listen to people, you can come up with more relevant and compelling responses to influence them into taking action in the right direction.

I noticed this conversation where an enthusiastic and eager salesperson was trying to sell something to my friend. He launched into an impressive pitch about how the product would fulfill a clear want, and make things easier for my friend. However, at the end of the sales pitch, my friend mentioned how he wasn't really keen on buying the product right away because he was considering buying a similar product from another company and wanted to analyze competitor products before making a purchasing decision.

It is amazing how the salesperson just switched off beyond the point where my friend mentioned he wasn't considering buying the product just yet. He completely missed the part about competitor products and hence didn't do what a person would've logically done in such a situation – launched into a comparison about how his product offered more value in comparison with the competitor's product. You can come up with compelling responses and hit the nail on the hammer if you listen to people.

Always acknowledge a person through verbal and non-verbal clues so they know you are keenly listening to them. It can be nodding in agreement or sending out verbal expressions such as hmmm and ahhh. You can ask questions about what they said to reveal that you've been listening to them or simply paraphrase what they said to reveal your understanding. For example, "Pete, if I understand you correctly, you are upset with our organization because we haven't met your expectations of good customer service, is that correct?"

This can be followed with an empathetic statement such as, "I totally understand how you feel, and I'd feel the same too if I was in your place." This works especially well when the other person is irate or disturbed about something. You aren't just listening to them but also assuring them that it's normal to feel what they are feeling. This helps them drop their defensive guard almost immediately.

Avoid interrupting a person when he or she is speaking. Hold on until they finish before adding your inputs. Also, don't always launch into a solution offering mode. Sometimes, people are not looking for a solution. They already know the solution or the lack of it. All they seek is someone to listen to them. Sometimes, the urge to offer solutions is so overpowering that we end up disrupting the speaker's flow when all he/she wants is to be heard.

It is a general tendency to switch off when a person has been speaking for too long. To show your keenness and attentiveness, ask questions or repeat the last few words to enable the speaker to know that you are indeed listening to him or her.

Another important point is to listen to people with an open and receptive mind. You may not always agree or identify with what they are saying. It may not be something you relate to. However being open and flexible to the other person's view is at the heart of being a good listener! Be and open and non-judgmental listener, which will make you more endearing to people. Agree to disagree respectfully when you don't necessarily agree with the other person's perspective.

Understand where they are coming from, and without jumping to quick conclusions.

I just can't stand sentence grabbers, and I am pretty sure it the same with everyone else except the sentence grabbers themselves. Some people are slow thinkers and speakers. They take time to create thoughts and ideas, and express them. Avoid the urge to finish their sentences for them or hijack the conversation. It will make you come across as someone who just doesn't give others a chance to speak and is constantly looking to hog the limelight, which isn't a very flattering impression.

I am sure each of us one such person is our life who is always looking to complete other people's sentences for them. Try to understand people before showing your smartness, and leading them on another thought trail. Keep your senses completely alert while the other person is talking. Allow their thoughts, ideas and feelings to form a mental visual by staying focused on what they are saying. Focus on the keywords/phrases and words they use repetitively throughout the conversation. It will help you use this information to persuade them into doing what you want them to.

Chapter Nineteen:
Repetition Is the Key

This works wonders when it comes to communicating with a subject's subconscious mind. Once you successfully embed a message in the subject's subconscious mind, it is easier to influence them into doing what you want. People may make decisions consciously. However, these decisions are largely driven by their subconscious mind, a fact even they aren't aware of. To use this technique and persuade a person on a subconscious level, the idea is to keep repeating certain powerful words and phrases.

You know how positive affirmations work, right? It is a series of powerful and motivating statements that we repeat several times throughout the day. The idea is to lead out subconscious mind into believing that we are indeed happy, healthy, prosperous, successful and whatever else you want to be. Once the subconscious mind believe this to be your reality, it will direct or guide your actions in line with this thought process. Thus feeding ideas into a person's subconscious mind is one of the most powerful ways to get them to do what you want. How do you accomplish this?

Repeat certain keywords and phrases so these ideas are firmly imprinted into the subject's subconscious mind. Our conscious mind may not be very focused because it is constantly dealing with an information overload. However, our subconscious mind seldom misses anything, especially if it is said repetitively. Once the subconscious mind accepts something as true, it is easier to get a person to make a decision in your favor. The human subconscious mind is a highly potent tool of influence because it seldom forgets anything.

Lets us consider an example to understand this even better. Let us say you are trying to get a person who is low on ambition and drive to apply for a job. You want them to be all inspired and charged up about doing well in their career but you also know that they are low on ambition and not receptive to idea of taking up a full-time job. You have to use the right keywords and phrases without being too straightforward. Your keywords can be duty, rewards, money, better life, travel, lifestyle, good education for children.

You are sowing seeds in their subconscious mind without directly saying, "Loser, just get up and get a job before you lose everything you have." Even though this is the reality, you have to plant the idea in their subconscious mind subtly so it leads them into action, and prevents them from resisting it. Use one or two powerful keywords related to the action or emotion you want to evoke. Repeat it several times during the conversation to connect with subject's subconscious.

This technique doesn't show instant results simply because you are working with a person's subconscious mind. It takes time for the message to sink into the subconscious mind and manifest. However, this works wonders on a long-term basis because once you feed something into a person's subconscious mind, it is almost never forgotten.

One of things to safeguard against while using this strategy for influence or manipulation is to never make it obvious to the subject that you are trying to feed certain ideas into his or her subconscious mind. If the person realizes that you are trying to manipulate him or her, the entire strategy will fall flat. They will become non-receptive and defensive to what you are saying, which you clearly don't want.

There really is no thumb rule for the number of times you must repeat a keyword for it to work. The idea is to say it as many times as you can. However, make sure that it is done in a subtle and unnoticeable manner. You may want to work with different keywords that convey the same meaning to avoid getting noticed for using the same keyword over and over again, which can arouse your subject's suspicion.

Though you are changing your words, the meaning essentially stays the same. There is reduced risk in being discovered by using different words and phrases to send the same signal into a person's subconscious mind.

Stick to simple and relevant keywords. This simply means that the subject should be able to connect these keywords with what you want them to do. Some words may have highly subjective connotations.

For example, specific colors may signify different things to different people. You may want to romance a person, and hence to instill romantic feelings about you in their subconscious mind, you may use the color red in your conversation very often. To them, red may signify danger, anger and aggression. For you, it may be rose, to them it is the color of blood. Thus, avoid using subjective keywords or phrases that may have different connotations for different people and opt for more universal words and phrases. Find universal keyword to communicate the idea you want to, and use it to establish a connection with your subject's subconscious mind in the most effective manner.

Chapter Twenty:
Use the Power of Your Voice

Whether you realize this or not – your voice can totally make or break what you are trying to say. Just before you are about to deliver an important speech or make a presentation, allow your voice to relax into its optimal pitch. If you want to come across as authoritative or want people to take you seriously, keep your tone low and steady rather than squeaky. Avoid raising your intonation towards the end of a sentence. It gives the impression that you are asking a question or are doubtful of something rather than making a statement.

It leaves the other listener feeling that you aren't sure of what you said or doesn't make you come across as convincing. For speaking with greater conviction, always keep a flat intonation towards the end of the sentence. End on a more assertive note, like you are making a convincing statement or pronouncing a statement.

Use the authoritative arc to your advantage. The authoritative arc is where your voice starts on a low note, then assumed a high note/ pitch in between the sentence, and then concludes on a low note again. Try using this when you are communing something important or addressing audience. You'll come across as more persuasive and authoritative.

Learn to control your tone if you want to be taken seriously. When we experience a surge of feelings and emotions, there is a visible lack of steadiness and consistency in the voice. Your feelings will be more conspicuous to people, which may not work to your advantage. Irrespective of the emotions you are undergoing, your voice shouldn't reveal anger, nervousness, disillusionment and other similar feelings. Learn to keep it steady and controlled to avoid giving away clues about your emotions.

If your feelings and emotions are obvious to the other person, they will end up cashing in on it rather than the other way around. Look for these clues in your subjects to better understand how they are thinking and feeling.

Again, the word your subject emphasizes on lends more meaning to what they are trying to communicate. For example, let us take a sentence such as, "Did you steal my shoes?" This is a simple question, but word emphasis can dramatically change its meaning. If the person emphasizes on you, it can reveal that the person is asking whether you stole it or someone else did. Similarly, by emphasizing of steal, they may be trying to establish whether you stole it or just borrowed it with the intention of returning it.

Again, if the subject emphasizes on shoes conveys that the person is trying to ask if you stole the shoes or something else. A change in the word you emphasize on can totally alter the meaning of a sentence or question. In addition to molding your voice to emphasize on the right words, watch out for the words other people emphasize on to know what they are trying to communicate. It will lend greater clarity and perspective to the communication, and lead you to take the required action.

You know how popular radio personalities animate their voices to have the desired impact on their audience? Learn to give more character to your voice when you are attempting to evoke certain emotions in your listeners. One of the most ineffective communication patterns is to speak in a standard tone. Yes, keep your voice and tone steady but don't hesitate to raise and lower the pitch at will to stir up the required emotions in your audience. Use your voice to deliver the right histrionics.

Always speak in an audible tone, and keep the rate of your speech medium paced. Sometimes people talk so fast (this is especially the case with quick thinkers who talk fast to keep up their pace of thinking) that they come across as nervous, emotional, anxious and unsure. Similarly, if you speak slowly, you will give the impression of being someone who can't gather their thoughts or has difficulty expressing themselves in a convincing manner. To be a master influencer, persuader, manipulator and leader, you must speak with a medium pace. Speak in a loud, coherent and clear manner.

Chapter Twenty-One:
Use the Right Words

There are certain words and phrases that can trigger your subjects hot buttons during verbal communication. These hot buttons or powerful words can be extremely effective when it comes to persuading, influencing or manipulating people by accessing their subconscious mind. Our subconscious mind links certain words/phrases with specific emotions, which in turn drives them to take action in the desired direction. Some words and phrases have deep psychological connotations, which can be used to your advantage.

If you want to lend greater credibility and positivity to what you are saying and get the other person to trust you, use words such as "genuine", "authentic", "legitimate", "valid", "trust", "assurance", "hope" and "love." People tend to respond more positively to these terms because they instill a sense of trust, warmth and security. You may get a person to trust you even more by using these terms. Notice how a majority of these terms are commonly used by internet marketers in their sales copy to lead their prospective customers into buying their products or services. A lot of these words feature prominently in direct sales copies.

Using these words and phrases is like verbally hypnotizing a person into doing what you want them to do. When you want a person to take immediate action, use terms such as right away, quickly, instantly, right now, immediately and other words that imply the same meaning.

These words are proven to create the required effect when it comes to getting people to take action without wasting time because they are known to leave a dramatic effect on our subconscious mind, which leads us to take immediate action.

Avoid filling gaps in conversations with terms such as "ummmm" or "aaaahhh." It makes you come across as an ineffective speaker who is unable to put their point across in a convincing manner. Nix these conversation fillers to make your talk more impactful, powerful and persuasive.

Always pause to create the desired impact when you've just made a crucial or dramatic point. Let the importance of what you've spoken be digested by the listeners. Avoid using words such as "actually", "really" "like" "mainly" etc. if you want to be taken seriously by the listener. The redundant terms will kill the impact of your speech.

Look up the pronunciations of words you aren't sure of. This is vital when it comes to establishing authority. People are less likely to take a person seriously if they pronounce words incorrectly. If you aren't sure about saying a word correctly, drop it. As an effective manipulator, attempt to learn at least 2-3 new words a day to be incorporated into your speech! It becomes simpler to manipulate or influence a person into doing what you want them to if you use articulate and appropriate expressions. Being an effective verbal communication is integral to being an expert influencer.

Make your discussions and arguments more impactful by sticking to compelling, effective and simple language.

Chapter Twenty-Two:
Establish Authority in a Domain

Another arsenal in your influencer kit is to establish your expertise or authority in a domain if you want people to take you seriously and do what you want them to. Cash in on your knowledge to make the most of a negotiation, presentation, business association or even personal/ social relationships. If you are a subject matter expert, flaunt your knowledge to build trust and credibility. If people realize that you truly know what you are saying, they will be more likely to go by your word or do what you tell them to.

The more people think you know about a subject or topic, the more likely will they be to trust what you say. Don't leave any opportunity to present yourself as an expert. Keep yourself updated with the latest trends in your industry. Don't allow your subject to gain an upper hand in the conversation. You should be in control and command of the conversation. If the topic veers in a direction you don't want it to, gently bring it back to your subject of expertise by saying something like, "getting back to stock market trends, I see a huge surge in the price of xyz."

This manipulation technique may require plenty of reading, preparation and practice, especially if you are not an expert on the matter and only pretending to be one to impress or influence the subject. Have all your research and analysis in place before meeting the subject. Talk to a real expert who can share his or her insights on the matter. You'll have most answers ready should the subject question you about something. Your knowledge and eloquence should instill confidence in the subject.

Use your expertise to make a person feel at ease with what you ask them to do. A person will most likely switch off from your suggestions (however well-meaning they appear) if he or she thinks you lack knowledge. However, if she or she is convinced of your expertise, the chances of them obeying you will increase. What's more? They may even ask for suggestions and advice. Grab this chance to get them to do what you want.

Master manipulators are implicitly trusted by people owing to their display of knowledge. Even if you aren't an expert, make an attempt to gain as much knowledge about what you are talking to present yourself as an expert. This doesn't make the other person feel like he or she is being manipulated. They get the feeling that you are simply sharing more information with them and even offering well-meaning advice.

What you are actually doing is entering their mind to gain greater control of their thoughts in a rational and logical manner. Through knowledge, you are shaping their opinion, thoughts and perspective.

Chapter Twenty-Three:
Reciprocity

Use the psychological principle of reciprocity to get a person to do as you say. It's a simple technique yet works brilliantly on a subconscious level.

What happens when a person does you a favor? You constantly live with the feeling of being obliged to it and feel the need to return the favor as soon as possible, right? Well, at least most people do. You feel like you owe them until the favor is returned. Psychologically, when a person does you a favor he or she gains a sort of psychological superiority over you. They have an upper hand during any interaction. It isn't obvious or they won't go around ordering you. However, subconsciously you both know they are above you. Use this subconscious psychological technique to your advantage.

Do the subject a favor, and make them feel obliged towards you. This will give you a psychological advantage that you can cash in on at the right time. When you tell someone who feels obliged towards you to do something, they are less likely to refuse. You wield more influence and power over them. Take for instance; you give someone a friend an expensive present on their birthday. After a couple of months, you ask them to buy something from you; do you think they will refuse? Slim chances! Reason – the friend feels obligated to you after you give them an expensive gift. He or she will find it near impossible to refuse your request.

Use this leverage wisely. Once you give something to someone or do them a favor, don't immediately accept a favor from them. This levels the equation. Refuse to take anything in return until the right moment when you want to get them to do what you want. Wait for the right time to cash in on the favor.

Similarly, when the subject thanks you for doing them a favor, don't say something like, "Oh, it isn't much really" or "It isn't a huge deal, don't mention it" Rather psychologically put it in their mind that they are obliged to you, and they will also do something similar for you in future. Say something like, "Oh, wouldn't you do the same thing for me? Of course, you would. Don't thank me for it, please." See what we did there? We simply planted the idea in their mind that they will do something for us if we need it too. Thus, we are subconsciously sowing the seeds for them to return our favor in future. Use subtle and clever words that make them feel obliged without them realizing that you are making them feel obliged.

Chapter Twenty-Four:
Be Honest and Genuine

If you want to influence people positively, be honest and sincere. You come across as credible when you are truthful and transparent. People are likelier to buy what you say. For instance, I know salespersons who make plenty of sales by being genuine and telling their potential customers about the upside and downside of their products. They won't just talk about the positives but also inform their customers about certain limitations of the product. These are small yet effective things that can make you an effective persuader. The best part is, you don't have to memorize things if you are honest. Genuine persuaders stick to facts, and offer a good perspective of a thing. This inspires their subjects' trust.

Yes, while lying and being dishonest can help you manipulate a person temporarily, it's not going to be an effective long-term strategy. For example, you lie to a potential customer about a product or service just to sell it, he or she will discover it sooner or later, and stop buying things from you. This means, you may a few quick sales in the beginning using trickery but it won't hold you good for a long haul. To influence people powerfully in the long run, it is always good to stick to the truth. Once people discover you lie to them, manipulating them in future is almost impossible.

Think about it this way. A salesperson doesn't mention any negative qualities whatsoever about product or service that he or she is selling.

After a point of time, won't you start doubting him or her? Now, think of another salesperson who mentions the pros and cons of a product or service to help you make a buying decision. Aren't you likelier to buy from a person who has stated upfront all the positives and negatives of the product or service for helping you make more informed choices?

Manipulators and persuaders make it highly complicated at times. They obsess over what to say and what not to say to make their subject perform the desired action. However, stop focus on putting up an act or contriving the truth. It is easier to stick to the truth than spin lies and lose trust.

Even if you make gentle and persuasive suggestions, ensure you back it up with solid facts and reasoning. Again, people are wary of being fooled and misled by people, which will shut them to what you are saying after a point of time if you are only speaking in glowing terms. Talk about both sides, present facts that can be verified and come up with valid arguments if you want people to have faith you or listen to you.

Make the solution you want people to take practical, logical and attractive. It should be packaged well but also truthfully. Don't make tall or lofty claims. People will be disappointed. Always attempt to under promise and over perform. This will make it come across as more genuine for your subjects. Earning the trust of your subjects is the most important aspect of persuading them or getting them to do what you want.

Your objective should be to get people to do what you want in the long-term not just couple of times. You risk losing their help in future if you trick them into short-term gains.

Chapter Twenty-Five:
Be Charismatic

If you ask me what exactly charisma is, it is hard to explain. It's a sort of attractiveness or magnetism that draws people to you. It the aura or persona you carry that attracts people to you like magnets. Manipulators or persuaders have plenty of charisma. People notice them as soon as they walk into a room. Though it's hard to explain charisma, it is easy to notice. You know it when you spot it. A majority of world leaders who possess the power to influence people radiate plenty of charisma. They are attractive, confident, positive and have well-developed influencer qualities.

Most leaders, salespersons, political figures and public personalities are constantly working on their charisma to come across as more confident and attractive. You should display a warm, amiable and friendly vibe. Use more open, trustworthy and positive language. Use impeccable manners and courtesy to win over people. Be hypnotic in your words and actions. Practice small talk to make a positive first impression on people. Come across as an interesting and arresting personality. Sweep people off their feet when you meet them and talk to them so they are instantly impressed with you.

When you are meeting people for the first time, read the day's latest news to sound informed. Talk about something funny that happened during the day. It'll break the ice, and make you come across as instantly likeable and relatable. The idea to win people over and persuade them is come across as more relatable. When people can relate to you, it'll be easier for them to do what you tell them to. Coming across as more human and relatable is the key to being able to influence people.

Don't we all take the suggestions and recommendations of our friends seriously? When they ask you to try a new restaurant in town, you will be likelier to do it than if someone comes and promotes it to you like a salesperson. Why? Because they are recommended by people you can relate to. You feel they are one of you, and if they find something appealing or good, you'll find it good too. Make yourself come across as accessible and relatable.

Confidence is the highlight when it comes to persuading people to do what they want. When you are sure and poised about what you are speaking, your subjects are able to make a decision in your favour more confidently. It reassures people about the idea that they are making the right decision. When you have faith in what you are doing, it easy to pass on this faith to others.

For instance, let's say you have a business plan and are looking for funding for the business. You have to make a presentation before associates who are responsible for providing the funding for your business. However, you come across as hesitant and unsure about the business. You don't look like you have too much conviction in the plan yourself. You can't answer questions posed to you by the associates. Do you think they will buy your business plan or have conviction in it?

Chapter Twenty-Six:
Stay Unpredictable

Do not allow people to be able to read you or predict your next move. If they are able to spot a pattern in actions, behavior, thoughts and personality, you will be manipulated instead of the other way around. There should be an element of mystery involved. People shouldn't know your next move. Being too open, transparent, and predictable will make you come across as a boring person, which doesn't do too much to add to your likeability factor. Don't always do what is expected out of you. Break the pattern at times and do something unexpected, unpredictable and out of the way.

You come across as more interesting, exciting and stimulating if you remain unpredictable. People will be on their toes to keep up with you. Staying unpredictable increases your value, and keeps people hooked to you. Don't we all love people who do something off beat, unique and unexpected? Keep people interested in you by doing new and different things. This way they'll find you more interesting. When you come across as more interesting and likeable, they are likelier to do what you ask them to. Don't let people predict your next move or set expectations about your behavior. Do something unique, unpredictable and unexpected frequently.

For instance, if you are dating someone, instead of going the chocolate, flowers and greetings route, pen a book of poems for them or make personalized gifts. It will make you come across as a more interesting and exciting partner. Everyone loves some amount of novelty in their life. It brings an element of freshness, and keeps things from staying boring and predictable. When you come across as interesting and exciting, you become more likeable. This increases your chances of getting people to do what you want them to.

All the same, don't stay unpredictable all the time. Otherwise the element of unpredictability will also lose its value. People may get tired, and worse may think you are doing it purposely. They may not take you seriously or worse may realize that you are using it as a manipulation technique. When you are influencing or manipulating someone, the golden rule is they shouldn't realize they are being influenced or manipulated. Use the element of unpredictability to add freshness once in a while. It'll keep things from following an old and predictably boring pattern.

People always like to associate with those who are interesting, and can keep things fresh and exciting. Unpredictability can be in anything from having a never before conversation to having a perspective different from the one you've always had. Be an interesting and unpredictable conversationalist. Avoid giving the impression that you are trying to bring attention to yourself. This won't make you come across as a very credible or trustworthy person. This technique is about making people do what you want by coming across as more interesting. It isn't about coming across as scheming and annoying. If you do something fresh and out of the ordinary, chances are people will like you more. This likeability can be used for getting them to take the desired action.

Once people notice your or appreciate your interesting persona, it is easy to establish a connection with them. Once you establish a rapport or connection with them, it is easy to get them to obey you. This can be used in combination with other manipulation techniques to make it even more successful. The idea is to get your subjects to notice you, and like you enough to do what you tell them to. They will be hooked to listening to you or following your actions once they notice that largely, your behavior, actions, thoughts and personality isn't dominated by a pattern. It just lends more excitement to your persona!

Chapter Twenty-Seven:
Distraction

This is another effective social manipulation strategy that is extensively used by leaders, political parties, governments, corporate head honchos and public personalities to distract attention from the main issue and get people to do what they want. To keep the main issue from away from the public or people's psyche, their attention will be diverted to trivial and unimportant issues constantly. This way people are focused on unimportant and irrelevant issues that really don't matter! It is a technique to keep people from focusing too much on the primary issue.

The manipulator or influencer successfully diverts the subject's attention to a matter that isn't of much consequence to cover up an important manner. It is done with the intention that the person's attention should not be fixated on thinking negative things about the main issue to such an extent that it may impact the manipulator negatively.

For example, if there is unrest within a company or organization about unfairly giving people the pink slips or laying them off unethically, the company may come up with shocking stories of personal scandalous or office romances to divert attention from the main topic of unfair layoffs. When leaders can do nothing to resolve issues, they simply choose to manipulate people by diverting attention from the issue.

Observe how political and world leaders will rake up issues in the middle of a huge calamity to divert focus from the main issue. People's attention span is very limited, and by raking up another scandalous or shocking issue, you simply shift the subject's focus on something else so they do what you want them to, and you don't face the negative impact of the larger issue. Diversion of issue works when you can't come up with a constructive solution for an issue.

Chapter Twenty-Eight:
Compliment People

Flattery is another wonderful manipulation technique that drives a person to do what you want then to. It is a great ice- breaker and makes the other person feel comfortable in your presence. It also makes you come across as more likeable and affable, which is the key to inspiring a person's trust.

When you meet a person for the first time (or any number of times for that matter), offer then a compliment. Ensure the compliment is sincere or genuine otherwise it's going to come across as fake flattery, which puts people off. Offer then an honest and heartfelt compliment and they'll be swept off their feet in no time.

Also, one of the golden rules for making compliments work is to make them specific. This makes it sound more natural and genuine than forced flattery. For instance, don't just say something boring such as, "you look beautiful." Rather day something like, "red is totally your color, you look elegant is this outfit" or "you have soulful eyes that speak volumes" or "your smile reaches your eyes, it's just so beautiful." Get into specifics while complimenting people.

"Those hive steps you do look so graceful" sounds more genuine and specific than "you are an amazing dancer." It lends more authenticity to your compliment. This will only come with practice and observation. Observe people carefully to find something unique, specific and good about them. Once you discover it, don't hesitate to share it with them.

It will instantly increase your likeability factor and help you build a rapport with people. People love being told what they are good at, and they instantly take to people who can see the good in them. When someone says something nice about you, you instantly feel a boost of positivity. This makes you like the person who complimented you, thus increasing their chances of getting you to do what you want them to.

Chapter Twenty-Nine:
Remember People's Names

If you've read Dale Carnegie's *How to Win Friends and Influence People*, one of the most important points mentioned by the ace self-help coach and motivational speaker is memorizing people's names and addressing them by their names as much as possible. This again works at a very subconscious and psychological level.

When people address their subjects by their name, it increases the familiarity factor. It makes the other person think that he or she knows me well or is one amongst my people. It helps establish a rapport at the subconscious level, which is very powerful. You develop an unknown connect with people when you address them by their name. It makes the interaction more personal and relatable, even if it is in a professional set-up.

Everyone wants a personal touch in things, and keep it human and relatable. Remembering people's names is therefore the key to being a magnetic and influential leader or persuader. Addressing people without their name makes them come across as just another number, which is mechanical and clinical.

Make a conscious effort to remember people's name of you really want to sweep them off their feet. Imagine meeting someone just once and asking their name. Remember it by repeating it a few times during the course of your conversation. Next time you meet the person, go for the kill and address them by their name.

Always call out to people with their names. If you find it tough to remember long and complicated names, break it up into sounds that make sense For example, if it's a Japanese name like Ayumi, you break the sounds into something more relatable and connection worthy with a high recall value such as "are you me."

This trick makes it easy to remember unfamiliar names. Repeat people's name a few times while interacting with them. This makes the subconscious mind connection even stronger. You connect with people on a psychological level, which is long term and more effective.

They'll be pleasantly surprised. Most people forget names and don't expect you to remember it either, especially if you've met them only once. They will instantly like you and once they like you, there are higher chances of them doing exactly what you want to them to. Find opportunities to address people by their name in a bid to establish a connect with them.

Each time you see them, greet them by using their name instead of simply saying hello or hey there. It will add more meaning to the interaction and set the rhythm for a more fulfilling relationship. People will be likelier to remember you if you address them by their name, and that's a huge plus when it comes to influencing people.

Your subject will meet several people like you during the course of his or her day to day interactions. However, what will make you stand out is the human element. The way you establish a connection with people in the beginning determines your future interactions and the way they relate to you to do what you want them to.

When you are introduced to people for the first time, go over everyone's names when you are not doing anything. This will help you practice remembering their names when you actually have to use it.

Chapter Thirty:
The Bitter Pill

Presenting something as a bitter pill that has to be taken in the absence of any other alternative is another clever manipulation tactic. At times, you'll have to present something as a bitter pill that is unavailable is a smart way to get people to do what you want them to or something they wouldn't otherwise do.

Let us assume, you want your employees to put in extra hours at work because you have to step up to be ahead of the competition, they may not agree. However, if you present it as a do or die situation where the market is really bad and companies that have to survive should up their game or risk not getting any client orders, thus shutting shop and rendering people unemployed, people may relent. The fear of losing their job may make your employees come around. You may add information about companies that had to shut down owing to lack of business and high operational costs.

If you realize your job is at stake, you will go the extra mile. You see how the manipulator plays here? The decision is being packaged as something that isn't pleasant yet absolutely necessary, so there's no way you can refuse. This technique makes it tough for the other person to refuse what you want them to.

You don't give the person any other choice, and lead them into believing that there's no other way. Basically, lack of any option makes them comply with what you want them to do.

Chapter Thirty-One:
Make Your Own Techniques

Manipulation or persuasion is a subtle art that has to be practiced and acquired over a period of time. There cannot be a one size fits all approach. Different manipulation techniques will work differently on different people. At times, based on the personality of a person or your analysis, you'll have to create an entirely new manipulation technique that works well for his or her personality. You'll never know what works and what doesn't until you try using it on people.

Experiment, be resourceful and develop your own techniques. Be prepared to make adjustments and modifications to the techniques mentioned in the book. As long as you get the basics right, you can make changes based on what works for you. You'll have to be a decent people reader or analyzer to know what will work for a certain person and what will not.

For instance, inducing guilt and playing the blame game may work on someone with a more submissive and meek personality. However, a more confident and self-assured person may not fall for it. They may require a different approach such as logical reasoning or paying them a compliment. Some approaches will work better on some personality types than others. At times, you may have to combine two to three techniques to come up with your own combination that works! Learn to keep it flexible and adapt it according to the type of personality you are dealing with.

Stay open and learn as much about people as you can if you want to understand their thoughts, actions, ideologies and personalities. Stay non-judgmental and approachable. Embrace new ideas. Experiment by twisting knowledge you already possess.

Bonus Chapter:
NLP Manipulation Techniques

NLP or Neuro Linguistic Programming is a bunch of techniques and methods for boosting communication with multiple layers of the brain. It is an approach that brings together psychotherapy, self-development and communication. The creators of NLP Richard Bandler and John Grinder state that there is indeed a strong co-relation between behavior, language and our neurological functions, which can be used optimally for learning and self development.

When a person masters NLP, he/she is able to communicate fluently in the language best understood by our subconscious mind. He/she can re-program people's ideas, thoughts, principles and beliefs to his/her own advantage. This in turn gives the NLP practitioner the power to influence and manipulate people.

NLP training is conducted at multiple levels since it a complex discipline. However, to break it down at it basic level, NLP practitioners pay very close attention to their subjects or targets, including skin flushes, eye movements, pupil dilation (that even body language experts would otherwise miss) to know how they are processing information within their mind or the information type that is being processed.

We've all experienced NLP at some point in our life. Some songs remind us of specific life phases, and therefore become closely associated with dominant emotions during that phase of our life. Every time we hear the song or piece of music, our subconscious mind experiences similar emotions. The song becomes an emotional anchor for triggering specific feelings we want in a person.

Through careful observation, NLP experts can tell which brain side is most active or dominant in an individual. They can also tell which of their senses are most powerful. For instance, some people are more visual learners and absorbers, while other people are more auditory information processors. NLP practitioners are adept at catching signals about a person's thoughts through his or her eye movements.

After gathering the required information, NLP practitioners inconspicuously mirror their subjects' verbal and non verbal mannerisms to give them (subjects) the feeling that the practitioner is similar to them. NLP experts are also proficient in the art of offering false social clues to influence their subjects into dropping their guard to enter a more receptive, flexible and open state of mind. This makes it easier for the manipulator to persuade or influence their subjects into doing what they want.

NLP practitioners will carefully and purposefully use language that considers a person's most predominant senses. For instance, if you (manipulator) realize that his subject is a visual person, he/she will say things such as, "Can you see where I am coming from?" or "Do you see what I am trying to explain?" or "Look at it this way" If a person is more auditory, you can speak to them using a more auditory language such as "Hear me out before you say something" or "I completely hear out John."

NLP practitioners use NLP to establish rapport through smart use of body language, verbal patterns and other clues to help their subjects let down any resistance, and make their minds more moldable.

NLP experts attempt to achieve two objectives, eliciting and anchoring. Eliciting is when a subject is drawn into an emotional state of mind through the usage of emotional language. Once the desired state is achieved, the NLP practitioner will anchor that specific emotion with a physical cue. For instance, they will first draw you into a highly emotional state of regret, and then purposefully tap you on the shoulder.

Now, the NLP practitioner can trigger the same emotion of regret in you by gently tapping you on the shoulder. They cleverly combine an emotion with a physical clue, so they have greater control on invoking the same emotion in you through the use of that physical clue.

Let us take another example. The NLP expert makes you feel unworthy and depressed through the use of language. They follow this up with touching your palms in a specific way. Now each time they want to induce feelings of unworthiness and depression in you, they simply have to touch your palm. The manipulator is conditioning you to experience specific emotions connected with physical cues.

Apart from using the power of touch for anchoring emotions, NLP practitioners purposefully use vague and ambiguous words to induce a sort of hypnotic trance over their subjects. This is done to prevent their subjects from disagreeing with them or resisting their views. Thus, making it easier for the subject to give in to what you are saying. Barack Obama used the technique very effectively during the now famous "change" campaign. Change could be interpreted by people any way they wanted.

Again, NLP practitioners use language that is layered and lots of hidden meanings or different underlying connotations linked to it. They'll use popularly known information, while subtly slipping their agenda into the other person's subconscious mind for making it easier for them to think in a particular way. For example the manipulator may sneakily say, "Eating, sleeping and going out with me are the secrets of a good life."

On the face of it, it appears like you are sharing well-meaning tips to enjoy a healthier life. The person invariably agrees with this without thinking too much. However the multilayered, hidden message is, "going out with me." At a subconscious level, you got the other person to agree to what you are saying. This is a powerful, little-known and subtle NLP technique that is used by NLP practitioners to influence their subjects into agreeing to their ideas.

There is also another typical NLP trick of following a question with another one intended to create conditioning by association. For instance, you inquire with someone, "How many fingers do human hands have?" Obviously 10! How many fingers on ten hands? Most people will say 100. However, the correct answer is 50. As an NLP practitioner, you are creating an opening for your leading your subject to think the way you want them to through conditioning and association.

You build anchors or a baseline that allows you to take your subjects wherever and whenever you wish to a specific thought process or decision. It comes with training, learning and practice. Speaking about the association, it is extensively used by marketers and advertisers to connect specific products and services with certain lifestyle attributes, aspirations and lifestyles..

Conclusion

Thank you again for purchasing this book!

I genuinely hope this book was able to help you to understand the basics of manipulation, influence and persuasion, and can be used in your daily life.

The next step is to use all the strategies, tips and techniques used in the book to influence people's minds and persuade them into doing what you want them to without even knowing it.

The book is packed with practical actionable tips, and real life examples to help you develop a better understanding of the art of manipulation and how to implement it effectively to get people to feel, think and behave the way you want them to.

Finally, if you enjoyed this book, then I'd like to ask you for a favor, would you be kind enough to leave a review for this book on Amazon? It would be greatly appreciated!

Other Books By Leonard Moore

Manipulation

21 Proven Techniques To Secretly Manipulate, Persuade And Influence Anyone

Maybe you've been led to believe that brainwashing other people is something that can only happen in movies. Maybe you think that taking advantage of the subconscious mind is something only crazy people would try to do.

The truth is, as human beings we're imperfect. We have weaknesses. And if you study and get to know these weaknesses you'll have a huge power in your hands. When you master the right manipulation techniques, the real ones, it is completely possible to influence other people's thinkings and make them do what you desire.

In this book you'll find 21 of the best manipulation techniques, the ones that can easily give you access to almost anybody's mind. By learning and applying them, you will have the chance to create a great positive change in your life and reach your goals faster.

This handy manual will teach you:
- 21 Proven Techniques to Manipulate And Brainwash Anyone
- The Right Way To Disagree Without Sounding Disagreeable
- How To Interpret And Take Advantage Of Gestures
- Working Ways To Build a Relationship With Your Listener
- How To Mirror And Direct Others Without Anyone Noticing You
- Practical Strategies To Penetrate The Subconscious Using Keywords
- How To Set The Right Mood To Manipulate Others In A Conversation
- Common Mistakes And How To Avoid Them (The Majority of People Doesn't Know This)
- And much, much more

Learn how to get in control and live a life of happiness, success, joy, and peace.

"Manipulation" by Leonard Moore is available at Amazon.

Persuasion: The Psychology of Selling
Proven Techniques, Strategies And Scripts To Close The Sale Every Time

Sales may be about math, but the selling itself is based on psychology, understanding consumer mindset, and persuasion techniques.

The good news is, anyone can master the art of selling. It isn't a secret superpower that some people are just born with. It is a carefully cultivated and practiced skill that can help you in many situations in life.

We are all salespeople. We are either selling our best qualities to a new date or selling our expertise/experience to a prospective employer or selling our ideas to people or convincing our friend to join us for a weekend movie. Knowingly or unknowingly, we are all selling.

I'd say sales training is excellent training for social or public life. You meet new people every day, learn to handle objections, gain greater knowledge about the buyer's needs/psychology, look for a common ground, and handle rejection.

In this book you'll learn the best selling techniques and psychological strategies to close the sale every time. With the help of this guide, you'll be able to identify your target prospects, understand what drives people to make buying decisions, how to use emotions and facts to overcome objections and close the sale.

As a bonus, you'll also find two sample sales scripts that will show you how to apply the techniques learned in everyday life to improve your skills and sell more.

In this guide you'll learn:
- Proven Techniques To Close The Sale Every Time
- 9 Sales Techniques That Actually Work, Explained
- What Drives People To Buy And How To Take Advantage Of It
- How To Become A Superstar Salesperson
- How Psychology Can Help You Sell More
- 4 Rules To Be A Great Salesman
- The Best Strategies For Prospecting And Getting Appointments
- 10 Most Common Objections And How To Overcome Them
- Sample Sales Scripts That Show How To Apply The Techniques Described
- And Much, Much More

Discover how to close every sale!

"Persuasion: The Psychology Of Selling" by Leonard Moore is available at Amazon.

www.ingramcontent.com/pod-product-compliance
Lightning Source LLC
Chambersburg PA
CBHW072300260726
48658CB00002BA/507